The Missions of California

Mission Nuestra Señora de la Soledad

Kim Ostrow

The Rosen Publishing Group's
PowerKids Press™
New York

For Mom and Dad—to show their friends.

Published in 2000 by The Rosen Publishing Group, Inc.
29 East 21st Street, New York, NY 10010

First Edition

Book Design: Danielle Primiceri

Layout Design: Maria Melendez

Photo Credits and Photo Illustrations: pp. 1, 16, 30, 33, 41, 43, 45, 49, 50, 50a, 51, 51a © Shirley Jordan 1995 Soledad; p. 6, 20, 47 © The Granger Collection; p. 46 © Stock Montage; p. 4, 14 © SuperStock; pp. 10, 17, 19, 22, 23, 26, 27, 28, 29, 31, 32, 34, 40, 40a, 48, 49 © Christina Taccone; p. 8, 24 © Corbis-Bettmann; p. 52, 57 © Christine Innamorato; pp. 9, 12, 20, 36, 39 © Tim Hall; pp. 7, 11, 13 © Michael Ward.

Editorial Consultant Coordinator: Karen Fontanetta, M.A., Curator, Mission San Miguel Arcángel
Editorial Consultant: Karen Fontanetta, M.A.
Historical Photo Consultants: Thomas L. Davis, M. Div., M.A.
                              Michael K. Ward, M.A.

Ostrow, Kim.
    Mission Nuestra Señora de la Soledad / by Kim Ostrow.
       p. cm. — (The missions of California)
    Includes bibliographical references and index.
    Summary: Discusses the Mission Nuestra Señora de la Soledad from its founding to the present day, including the reasons for Spanish colonization in California and the effects of colonization on the Ohlone Indians.
    ISBN 0-8239-5500-1
    1. Nuestra Señora de la Soledad (Mission : Calif.)—History Juvenile literature. 2. Spanish mission buildings—California—Soledad Region—History Juvenile literature. 3. Franciscans—California—Soledad Region—History Juvenile literature. 4. Ohlone Indians—Missions—California—Soledad Region—History Juvenile literature. 5. California—History—To 1846 Juvenile literature. [1. Nuestra Señora de la Soledad (Mission : Calif.)—History. 2. Missions—California. 3. Ohlone Indians—Missions. 4. Indians of North America—Missions—California. 5. California—History—To 1846.] I. Title. II. Series.
F869.N8088 1999
979.4'76—dc21   99-23211
                                                         CIP

Manufactured in the United States of America

Contents

Spain Explores California

Mission Nuestra Señora de la Soledad

A mile west of the Salinas River lies a beautiful stretch of land that was once the shared home of Spanish friars, Ohlone Indians, and Salinan Indians. These groups of very different people lived together, worked together, and made history together. The friars and Indians were brought together because of a plan to bring Christianity and Spanish ways to California Indians. This plan was called the mission system, and Mission Nuestra Señora de la Soledad was one mission that played an interesting and unique role in that plan.

The Age of Exploration

The 1400s and 1500s were years of great exploration throughout the world. European explorers were eager to discover new lands in search of great treasures like gold and spices. Spain sent Christopher Columbus, who traveled the seas and discovered the New World (Central America, South America, and North America) in 1492. Spain was particularly interested in exploring North America and its western coast. At this time, many people believed that there was a river that ran through America, from the Atlantic Ocean to the Pacific Ocean. If such a river was found, it would mean that sailors could reach Asia faster and bring back riches like tea, silk, and spices to sell in Europe.

New Spain

In 1519, Hernán Cortés traveled to the land that is today Mexico. In 1521, he and his men conquered the great Aztec empire and claimed the Aztec lands for Spain. The Spanish called the lands New

◀ *Christopher Columbus traveled the seas exploring many areas of the world.*

▲
A missionary preaching to Indians.

Spain. They established a government there under a viceroy who would rule New Spain as a representative of the Spanish king.

Spain wanted to expand its empire even further. This meant not only claiming new land, but also gaining new Spanish citizens. The Spanish were Catholics (people who follow the teachings of Jesus Christ and the Bible). They knew there were many Indians living in the New World, and the Spanish wanted to teach them about Christianity. They wanted the Indians to give up their religion and convert to Catholicism. The Spanish felt that this was for the good of the Indians, since they believed that only Catholics went to heaven after death. Once converted to Christianity, the Indians would also become tax paying Spanish citizens.

The government in New Spain decided to send an explorer to Alta California to see if it would be a good place to settle. In 1542, an explorer named Juan Rodríguez Cabrillo was the first European to see the coast of Alta (meaning upper) California from the sea. Cabrillo sailed with three ships called the *San Salvador*, the *Victoria*, and the *San Miguel*. He was able to explore the areas now known as San

Diego Bay, Catalina Island, San Pedro, Santa Monica, and Ventura. Cabrillo met many Indians living along the coast. He discovered that they were friendly and peaceful. He traded different items with the Indians, mostly in exchange for food. After exploring these areas and claiming the land for Spain, Cabrillo and his crew ran into some stormy weather. They took shelter from the rough winds on San Miguel Island. Cabrillo died on San Miguel Island, but his crew

▲ *A Spanish friar teaching Indians about Christianity.*

continued on without him. Cabrillo's expedition was thought to be a failure by the government of New Spain because the explorers did not find a river passage through North America. However, many people today regard Cabrillo as the first explorer of the California coast.

Other Spanish expeditions sailed, but had no better luck in the search for a North American river passage. In 1602, a Spanish businessman and sailor named Sebastián Vizcaíno was sent by New Spain's rulers to find both harbors and areas to settle in California. Vizcaíno thought that if he did not bring home a good report, he would not get the rewards promised him, including the command of a large ship. He told officials in New Spain that Monterey Bay, which he named after the viceroy of New Spain, would make an excellent harbor, that the land had good timber, and that the American Indians living in the area were friendly. However, the viceroy of New Spain was still unsatisfied. He thought Vizcaíno had been unsuccessful because a waterway connecting the Atlantic and Pacific Oceans had not been found. Actually, no such waterway exists. The viceroy did not think the time or money invested in these trips was well spent, so Spain decided to stop funding these expeditions overseas. No Spanish ships sailed to California for the next 160 years.

Colonizing Alta California

Throughout these years, both Russia and England began sending ships to the Pacific coast of North America. Spain became concerned that they might lose the land that Cabrillo and Vizcaíno had claimed. Spanish rulers quickly decided that it was time to colonize Alta California and permanently control the land.

In 1591, Spain had sent a group of friars called the Jesuits to convert the Indians in New Spain to Christianity and make them Spanish citizens. The Jesuits founded many missions in New Spain, including the area called Baja (meaning lower) California (today known as the Baja Peninsula of Mexico). The Spanish government began to think that the Jesuits were too powerful and that they were hiding many riches that they had

Gaspar de Portolá and his crew exploring on horseback.

8

found in the New World. In 1767, the king of Spain ordered the Jesuits to leave the New World. He then sent a military captain named Gaspar de Portolá to act as governor in these new lands. Portolá did not find any riches in the Jesuit missions. In fact, the missions were poor and run down.

The Franciscans

Franciscan friars were sent to California to pick up where the Jesuits left off. Franciscans were a different order of Catholic friars. They followed the principles of a man named Saint Francis of Assisi. Franciscans wear woolen robes

A Franciscan friar wearing the traditional woolen robe.

cinched at the waist with a white cord. Their feet are bare, except for sandals. To join the Franciscan brotherhood, one must vow never to marry, never to seek material wealth, and to always act in total obedience to God. In order to make sure that the friars did not become too powerful, the Spanish government also sent soldiers to keep order. The soldiers lived in a separate military fort called a presidio. They were in charge of punishing anyone who broke the mission rules. This meant that the friars were free to focus on teaching the Indians.

The Ohlone Indians

The Ohlone Indians

Before the Spanish came to Alta California, there were already many different tribes of American Indians living there. A tribe called the Ohlone were living in the area between San Francisco Bay and Monterey Bay. They had lived there for more than 1,000 years before the Europeans arrived.

Living off of the Land

The Ohlone lived in villages. The number of people in a village was usually about 200. They lived in thatched huts that were made out of tule. Like many American Indian tribes, the Ohlone lived off the land that surrounded them. The most important part of the tribe's diet was acorns. For the Ohlone, the entire year was organized around harvesting acorns. The beginning of the year was counted from the first day that acorns were harvested. Acorns were gathered by everyone in the tribe. Then the women ground the acorns into flour and prepared a hot cereal similar to oatmeal.

The women in the Ohlone tribe also gathered berries, nuts, grapes, mushrooms, and roots. The men of the tribe fished and hunted for animals like deer, elk, otter, and rabbits. The Ohlone tribe was one of only a few California tribes that planted their own food. The Ohlone set fire to their fields to

Indian women used objects like this to grind their food.

Ohlone Indians lived in thatched huts. ▶

▲
The Ohlone were skilled fishermen.

get rid of weeds. Burning the fields was also important because it created grassy meadows. The meadows lured animals that could be hunted.

Clothing

In the warmer months, the men and children of the tribe did not wear clothing. The women wore aprons with a front and back that were made out of bark. They also wore caps that looked like baskets. These caps helped them carry heavy loads. In the winter, the Ohlone wore capes or blankets made out of animal hides. Rabbit fur or deer fur was often used, but otter fur was thought to be the warmest. Both men and women wore necklaces made out of stones and shells. Women sometimes wore grass or flowers as earrings.

Baskets

The Ohlone women were well known for their skill in basketmaking. Baskets were used for many different tasks such as collecting food and cooking. Ohlone baskets were so tightly woven that they could be used to store and transport water.

Religion

Before the Spanish arrived, the Ohlone had their own religion. They believed that there were spirits all around them. Different things in nature were thought to have spirits. The sun, for instance, was very important to the Ohlone. They would welcome the sun every morning with shouting and songs.

The Ohlone Indians had religious healers, or shamans. Shamans were believed to be closer to the spirit world than other people. Tribes had different shamans for different tasks. A shaman was believed to be able to control the weather, cure sickness, or predict if there would be a good harvest.

This is an Indian shaman.

The Ohlone had their own interesting culture, but when the Spanish arrived this changed forever. The effects of the mission system on the Ohlone people can still be seen. Today, the Ohlone language is no longer spoken and there are no full-blooded Ohlone Indians still living.

Understanding the Mission System

The Spanish and the Ohlone

The Spanish government's plan to convert the Indians to Christianity and make them into Spanish citizens would affect every aspect of the Ohlone culture. At the time when the missions were being set up in the New World, many people in Europe believed that the American Indians' culture was not very developed. Today, we know that the Indians had a culture that was different from the Spanish, but not worse. The California Indians had their own interesting and successful culture, one that had kept them productive and healthy for generations. The Spanish thought that they were helping the Indians by making them wear clothes, speak Spanish, and become Christians.

Another reason that the friars wanted to covert the Indians had to do with their desire to spread their religion. In the Catholic religion, it is believed that only Catholics go to heaven after death. The friars thought it was their job to teach other people about Christianity. They thought they were helping the Indians. A person who travels to other countries teaching people about Christianity, and encourages them to follow the teachings of Jesus Christ and the Bible, is called a missionary. An Indian who lived at the mission and converted to Christianity was called a neophyte.

Choosing a Mission Site

In order to start a mission, the friars would have to find a good location. Many different key elements were considered when choosing the mission site. A source of water, fertile soil, and plenty of wood were all necessary for founding a mission. Most important for the survival of

◀ *A missionary teaching Indians about Christianity.*

▲

This photograph shows the original site of the mission church.

the mission was a nearby Indian population because the missionaries would need the Indians' help to build and run the mission. Usually, a friar would form an expedition to search for a location. When he found the perfect spot, he would make a wooden cross and place it in the ground. Then, the friar would bless the site and hold the first Mass. Almost immediately, everyone at the mission would get to work. Soldiers would begin building temporary mission buildings. The friars would begin to look for California Indians to bring into the mission system.

The friars built this cross to mark the site of Mission Nuestra Señora de la Soledad.

The Founders of the California Missions

Fray Serra

The Jesuits had founded missions in New Spain and Baja California, but when they were ordered to leave, the missions were left without religious leaders. The Spanish government wanted to extend the missions even further, into Alta California. A strong and dedicated leader had to be found in order to accomplish these goals. That man was Junípero Serra.

Fray Junípero Serra was born on November 24, 1713, in the village of Petra on the Spanish island called Majorca. Serra's parents named him Miguel José Serra. Even though his parents were poor farmers, they believed in education and wanted their son to learn how to read and write. Miguel José decided at an early age that he wanted to dedicate his life to religion. At the local Franciscan friary, the friars taught him reading, writing, mathematics, and religious song. When Serra was 15, he went to school in the capital city, Palma. When Serra was 17, he joined the Franciscans. One tradition of the Franciscans is that a young man chooses a new name when he joins. Serra chose the name Junípero in honor of one of Saint Francis's most dedicated followers. Junípero Serra became a teacher at the school in Palma for six years. Although he was a successful teacher, Serra's dream was to become a missionary. He wanted to bring Christianity to people in other countries.

In 1749, Serra and two of his former students, Francisco Palóu and Juan Crespí, had the chance to follow their dreams of becoming missionaries. Catholic friars were needed in New Spain. Even though the site was so far from home, and the men would probably never

A statue of Fray Serra, the father of the California missions. ▶

*A portrait of
Fray Serra.*

return to their homeland, the three were eager to begin this long journey.

When Serra first arrived in New Spain, he insisted on walking from Veracruz to the capital, Mexico City. This walk was 260 miles long! Serra was a small, frail man, but he was a hard worker. The three men spent 14 days walking to reach the college of San Fernando. The weather was very hot, and the wool robes the friars wore made it even hotter. The friars never complained. They believed that hardship was part of their life's work. One evening during their trek, Fray Serra got an insect bite on one of his feet. The bite became infected, and the pain spread throughout his leg. The men stopped their journey for a day while Serra rested. Although he told them he was fine and they continued on the next day, the pain in Serra's leg never left him and grew worse as he grew older. He walked with a limp for the rest of his life.

In January of 1750, Serra and his traveling companions reached Mexico City. He spent the next 17 years working for the College of San Fernando.

Baja California

In 1767, Fray Serra was selected to head 15 existing Spanish missions in an area of Baja California in what is today northwestern Mexico. Serra worked hard to make sure the missionaries were happy. Different Franciscan missionaries were in charge of running each individual mission, and Serra supervised them all. He often visited the missions to make sure the friars had everything they needed. One year later, Spain claimed all of Alta California for its own. Fray Serra's life changed forever.

When plans were discussed to start new missions in the uncharted Alta California, Serra was the obvious choice to head up this large and challenging project. Serra's lifelong dream came true. He would now travel to

This map shows the locations of the 21 missions along the California coast.

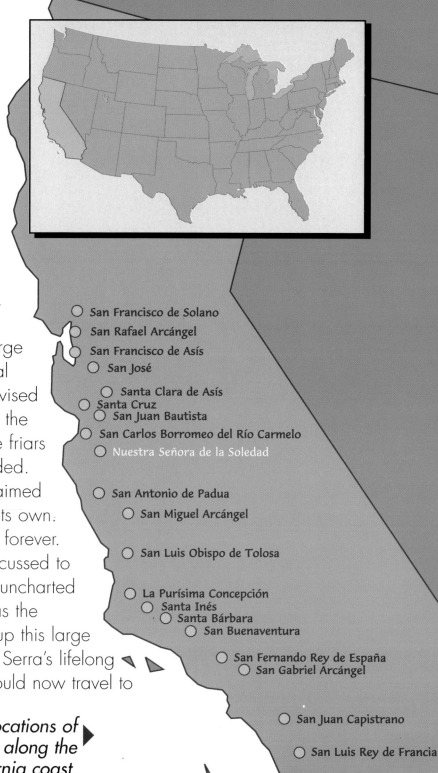

○ San Francisco de Solano
○ San Rafael Arcángel
○ San Francisco de Asís
○ San José

○ Santa Clara de Asís
○ Santa Cruz
○ San Juan Bautista
○ San Carlos Borromeo del Río Carmelo
○ Nuestra Señora de la Soledad

○ San Antonio de Padua
○ San Miguel Arcángel

○ San Luis Obispo de Tolosa

○ La Purísima Concepción
○ Santa Inés
○ Santa Bárbara
○ San Buenaventura

○ San Fernando Rey de España
○ San Gabriel Arcángel

○ San Juan Capistrano

○ San Luis Rey de Francia

○ San Diego de Alcalá

places never visited before, and do his missionary work.

Serra was involved in founding 9 of the first 21 California missions. He had help from others, including Gaspar de Portolá and Fermin Francisco de Lasuén.

The Journey to Alta California

In 1769, the viceroy of New Spain chose Gaspar de Portolá to lead a group into Alta California to establish the first settlements. Portolá sent two ships and two walking expeditions to San Diego. Fray Serra accompanied Portolá on one of the walking groups, which left in March of that year. The expedition was a very difficult one. About 300 people had started the journey, but half of them died before reaching San Diego. On July 16, 1769, Fray Serra founded California's first mission, Mission San Diego de Alcalá. Serra set a cross in the ground and began the first Mass. Each mission ended up being about one day's journey from the next. They were built along a road known as El Camino Real, which means "The Royal Highway." After accomplishing many of the goals he had set for himself and playing a key role in Spain's mission system in New Spain and California, Fray Serra died on August 28, 1784.

▲
Arches and designs made by the Indians at Mission Soledad.

Fermin Francisco de Lasuén

After Serra's death, a new president of the missions was named. In 1791, President Fermin Lasuén founded the 13th mission, Mission Nuestra Señora de la Soledad. Lasuén was similar to Serra in many ways. He was determined to spread the word of his faith and had also spent many years trying to achieve his dream of working as a missionary. Lasuén was 66 years old when he assumed the job of president. Like Serra, Lasuén had been in New Spain since his 30s. Lasuén was president of the mission chain for 18 years. He was also responsible for introducing a new style of architecture to the missions. Lasuén showed the

Fray Lasuén brought a new style of roof tiles to the mission.

friars how to create round roof tiles and wide arches. This style was very popular and became a lasting symbol of the mission era.

23

Founding Mission Nuestra Señora de la Soledad

Our Lady of Solitude

In 1769, when Juan Crespí and Gaspár de Portolá traveled up to Monterey, they camped in a valley near the Salinas River. They were looking for a site for the 13th California mission. It is said that some of the Ohlone Indians came to see them there, but the Spanish and the Ohlone could not understand one another's language. One of the Ohlone Indians kept saying something in his language that sounded like the Spanish word *soledad*, which means lonely. The spot did seem isolated and quiet. When the mission was founded, it was named Mission Nuestra Señora de la Soledad, for the Virgin Mary, who is sometimes called Our Lady of Solitude. This mission is often referred to as Mission Soledad.

Founding the Mission

In 1791, Fray Lasuén wrote to the friars at Mission San Carlos Borromeo. He told them that he was going to found a mission in the valley near the Salinas river and asked them to send some neophytes there to prepare for his arrival. A group of neophytes left Mission San Carlos Borromeo in September, carrying supplies for the new mission. These neophytes built a hut and altar out of sticks and mud.

On October 9, 1791, Fray Lasuén arrived at the site accompanied by soldiers, and by Fray Diego García and Fray Mariano Rubí, who would live at the mission. The friars brought the religious vestments and objects that were necessary for the founding ceremony. Fray Lasuén placed a cross in the ground and blessed it. Then he said Mass. This ceremony showed that the site was now sacred. Soon after the

Mission Soledad was named for the Virgin Mary.

25

◀ Mission Soledad during its restoration.

founding ceremony, Fray Lasuén left the mission. Fray García and Fray Rubí were left in charge.

Fray Rubí

There was much work to be done at Mission Nuestra Señora de la Soledad. A church had to be built, farming needed to begin, and the friars wanted to baptize the local Ohlone Indians and convert them to Christianity. Although Fray García was a hard worker, Fray Rubí was not.

Fray Rubí had come to New Spain from Spain in 1788. He and a friend of his, Bartolomé Gilí, went to the Franciscan college in Mexico City, the College of San Fernando. At school, the two friends caused a lot of trouble. They pretended to be sick so they could skip classes and sleep all day. They robbed the storerooms and stole the supply of chocolate that was meant to be shared among everyone. At night, they bothered the other Franciscans by banging on pots and pans to make noise and rolling balls down the hallways of the dormitory. They sneaked over the college walls to go out at night in the city.

In 1789, the Franciscan leaders at the college told Rubí and Gilí that they were in trouble and that they might have to leave the Franciscan Order. Rubí and Gilí apologized for their inappropriate behavior. They asked to be sent to the Alta California missions. The

Franciscan leaders were very forgiving. They thought that a change of environment and more challenging work might do the two young men some good. They agreed to let Fray Rubí and Fray Gilí go to Alta California.

Fray Rubí arrived in Alta California in 1790. He was first sent to Mission San Antonio de Padua, but one year later, he was transferred to the more isolated Mission Nuestra Señora de la Soledad.

A Slow Start

In Mission Soledad's first year, not much was accomplished. A temporary church was built of wood and covered with a mud and grass roof. Fray Rubí often said that he was too sick to work, and he argued with Fray García. By the end of 1792, the friars were only able to get 11 Ohlone Indians to convert to Christianity and live with them at the mission.

Fray Lasuén was not pleased with Fray Rubí, nor was he pleased with Mission Soledad's progress. Fray Lasuén wrote to officials in New Spain requesting that Fray Rubí be allowed to return home. Since Fray Rubí was always pretending to be ill, Fray Lasuén wrote that Fray Rubí was too sick to continue his life at the mission. Friars

This man demonstrates how the walls were made when the mission was being built.

usually had to serve for 10 years at the missions before they were allowed to leave. Spanish officials wrote back to Fray Lasuén saying that Fray Rubí would not be allowed to leave Mission Soledad until they saw a note from a doctor describing his illness. Fray Lasuén got a doctor to write a note and had Fray Rubí sent home.

▲ *An adobe wall at the mission.*

Fray Gilí

In 1791, when Fray Rubí was helping to found Mission Soledad, his friend Fray Gilí left New Spain to go to Mission San Antonio de Padua. After a year of service there, Fray Gilí was sent to Mission Nuestra Señora de la Soledad.

Fray Gilí hadn't changed his ways any more than Fray Rubí had. Fray Gilí hated his work and his life at the mission. He also pretended to be sick and did not get along with Fray García. Fray Lasuén had to write to the officials in New Spain about Fray Gilí, too. This time, Fray Lasuén said that Fray Gilí's only illness was his disgust for his work and for Alta California, and that there was no cure but to send him away. Spanish officials allowed Fray Gilí to leave Mission Soledad in 1794.

Visitors at Mission Soledad.

The Adobe Church

Progress at Mission Soledad was slow because of all the problems with Fray Rubí and Fray Gilí. Fray García was not popular either and was said to mistreat the neophytes. Not many neophytes lived at Mission Soledad, and little work was done. Although it took awhile, once the temporary wooden church was built, work began on a more permanent adobe church. The friars still only had temporary wooden huts to live in, but they were very religious men and believed that a permanent church was more important than homes for themselves.

The friars taught the neophytes how to make adobe by mixing mud, straw, and water. The neophytes mixed the adobe with their feet and then packed it into rectangular wooden molds to make bricks. The bricks were left to dry in the sun. Once dry, the finished bricks were stored for later use.

To make the church walls, the adobe bricks were stacked on top of one another and cemented together with mud. While several adobe churches at the other missions were finished in one or two years, the church at Mission Nuestra Señora de la Soledad took seven years to complete. This was because there were so few neophytes at the mission. The small church was finally finished in 1797.

Daily Life

Friars and Soldiers

Life at Mission Soledad was challenging for everyone. The friars and soldiers had to learn to live in new homes that were often uncomfortable and bare. They were far away from their Spanish homes, families, and culture and often felt isolated.

The area around Mission Soledad was windy, hot, and dry in the summer and very cold in the winter. This harsh weather made it difficult for the older friars assigned to live at the mission. Many complained of poor health. This was one of the reasons that so many friars asked to be transferred to other missions.

Many friars were not experienced at managing farms or being in charge of so many workers. This presented constant challenges. The friars had to make sure the neophytes did their work, that they got along with one another, and that they were content with their life at the mission. The friars were also responsible for teaching the neophytes the Spanish language and way of life, and the Catholic religion.

The Neophytes

Life for the Ohlone Indians changed a great deal when they became neophytes at Mission Nuestra Señora de la Soledad. When they lived in their villages, they had been free to hunt and gather, perform their own ceremonies, and do as they chose. At the mission, they had to obey the friars and follow a strict schedule.

▲ *The ring of the mission bell was once a familiar sound.*

Part of the mission as it looks today. ▶

The Daily Schedule

Most days at Mission Soledad began with the ringing of the church bells at 6:00 A.M. After the Indians awoke, they went to church for prayer. Breakfast was at 6:30. The neophytes ate a cereal made from corn, called *atole*.

After breakfast, the mission bells rang to signal that it was time for work. The Ohlone men worked at leather and woodcrafting as well as farming and blacksmithing. The women were responsible for preparing food. They learned how to make many Spanish foods, which they cooked for everyone at the mission. The Ohlone women also spun yarn, wove blankets and cloth, and made clothes, candles, and soap. The children helped with the work and had classes in Spanish and Bible studies.

At noon, the bells rang to call everyone to the midday meal. Everyone ate a lunch that consisted of a meat and vegetable stew called *pozole*. At 1:00 P.M. there was a short rest period called *siesta*. Then at 3:00 P.M., *siesta* was over and everyone went back to work.

Evening prayers were scheduled at 5:00 P.M., followed by some free time. During the free time, the neophytes talked, sang, danced, and played games. Women were supposed to go to bed at 8:00 P.M., and men went to bed at 9:00 P.M.

Before learning to make Spanish food at the mission, Ohlone women ground acorns to make flour.

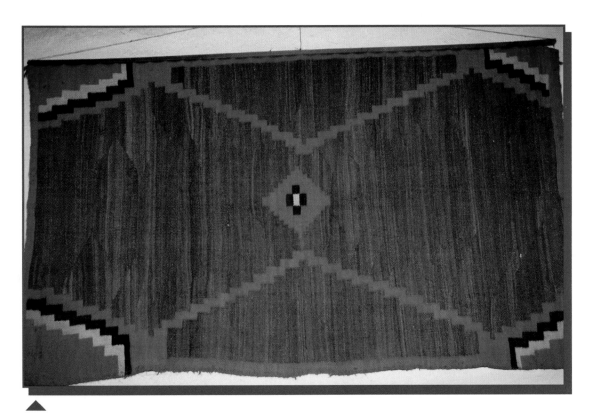

A beautiful blanket woven by Ohlone women.

Sucess and Challenge at the Mission

The Aqueduct

Fray García requested permission to leave the California missions and was allowed to go in 1797. He had served the full 10 years, first at other missions and then at Mission Soledad. In the early 1800s, the neophytes at the mission built an aqueduct under the supervision of a friar named Antonio Jaymé. The aqueduct was made of stone and was a system of channels that carried water from the Salinas River to Mission Soledad. The aqueduct was at least five miles long, and may even have been as long as 15 miles.

The aqueduct was very important to Mission Nuestra Señora de la Soledad. The weather in the area made it difficult to grow crops. Often it was very hot and dry, and crops died from the lack of water. At other times, the area would flood, washing away seeds that had been planted and killing crops that were already growing. The aqueduct allowed the people at the mission to have a steady supply of water from the river. Crops grew much better, and there was enough water for the livestock to drink. This improved life at the mission because there was more food. Because of this, more Ohlone Indians came to the mission and became neophytes.

The aqueduct also allowed everyone at Mission Nuestra Señora de la Soledad to bathe, wash clothes, and have fresh drinking water without ever leaving the mission. This made life easier and also encouraged more Ohlone Indians to live there.

◀ *The weather at Mission Soledad is often hot and dry.*

The Indians suffered much sickness and sadness from many diseases.

The Population Grows

Although work progressed slowly, farming, building, and ranching were all being done at the mission. Wheat and corn were planted and harvested. More and more nearby Ohlone Indians began joining the mission because Mission Soledad was able to produce a steady supply of food. By the year 1800, there were 512 neophytes living at Mission Nuestra Señora de la Soledad. The mission had 1,000 heads of cattle and 2,000 sheep.

Disease

Mission Soledad finally seemed like it was going to be a success, when in 1802, it suffered a terrible setback. An epidemic, thought to be smallpox, swept through the mission, killing many of the Indians. For a while, an average of six Indians died each day. Since the Indians had never been exposed to European illnesses like smallpox, they had no way to fight these deadly diseases. The population at the mission shrank even further because neophytes who were not sick ran away to escape the disease. When the epidemic ended, the people at Mission Soledad had suffered a great deal, but they were determined to go on.

A New Friar

In 1803, a friar named Fray Florencio Ibáñez came to Mission Nuestra Señora de la Soledad. Mission Soledad was a difficult place to be. It was not on the main road, El Camino Real, that connected most of the missions. Due to its out-of-the-way location, Mission Soledad did not get as many visitors as some of the other missions. The friars who served there often felt lonely and isolated. Over the 44 years that Mission Soledad was an active mission, 30 different friars served there. Some friars, like Fray Rubí and Fray Gilí, were sent away. Most of the others asked for permission to go to other missions. Fray Ibáñez was different. He stayed at Mission Soledad for 15 years, until his death.

Fray Ibáñez worked very hard to make Mission Soledad more successful. He wrote plays for the neophytes to perform at religious festivals, called *fiestas*. He was a good manager, and the neophytes liked him better than many of the other friars that came to and left the mission.

Other Mission Buildings

After the church was built at Mission Soledad, there were other structures that needed to go up. The mission buildings would be built in the shape of an open square called a quadrangle. Inside the quadrangle was a courtyard. The first building to be built after the church housed the friars' quarters, called the *convento*. The rest of the quadrangle would include living areas, a small guest area, kitchens, workrooms, and granaries. There were also two infirmaries, where the sick were cared for, one for men and the other for women.

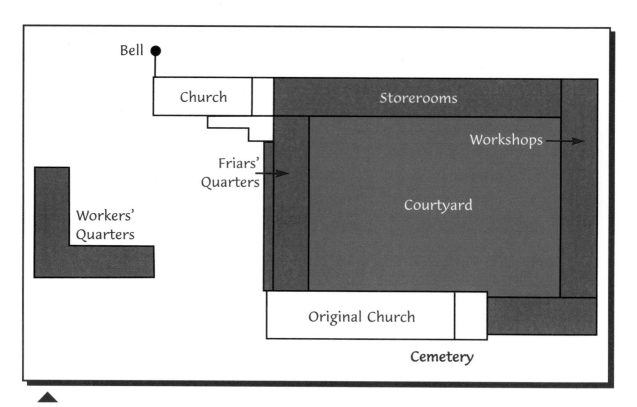

This diagram illustrates the layout of Mission Soledad.

Unmarried women and girls lived in a part of the mission quadrangle called the *monjerío*. They did much of their work there and were often not allowed to leave the *monjerío* until all of their work was done. At night, following an old Spanish custom, the women were locked in.

The rest of the neophytes lived in huts outside of the mission quadrangle. This neophyte housing was called the *ranchería*. Orchards and gardens were planted on the mission grounds. A cemetery, called the *camposanto*, was also near the mission church.

A New Church

By 1805, life at Mission Nuestra Señora de la Soledad was going so well that there were 727 neophytes living there. This was the greatest number of neophytes that ever lived at the mission.

Since the population was larger than when the earlier church had been built, Fray Ibáñez decided that the mission needed a new church. Work began in 1808.

Artwork showing an Indian plowing the land near the mission.

Sad Times

On July 24, 1814, an important visitor came to Mission Soledad. A good friend of Fray Ibáñez, named José Joaquín Arillaga, had become the governor of California. He was on a tour of all of the missions when he suddenly became very ill. He asked to be taken to Mission Nuestra Señora de la Soledad so that he could be with his old friend. Fray Ibáñez cared for Governor Arillaga as best he could, but the governor died two days later. He was buried beneath the church floor.

The mission received few other visitors until 1818, when a pirate named Hippolyte de Bouchard and his crew attacked the presidio at Monterey Bay. The pirates stole valuable property from the presidio and destroyed what they couldn't steal. Friars at nearby missions were afraid

▲

The altar in the church at Mission Soledad.

1818, at the age of 78.

that Bouchard would soon come after their missions. Mission Soledad was further inland than most of the other missions, so many friars, soldiers, and neophytes came to this mission for safety. When the friars heard that Bouchard had left the area, they got ready to go back to their missions. Before they left, they had to bury Fray Ibáñez, who died on November 26,

New Spain Becomes Mexico

In 1821, after 11 years of fighting, New Spain declared its independence from Spain and became known as Mexico. Alta California and all the California missions now belonged to the Mexican government. Because the Mexicans had just fought a war, they did not have much money to spare. Money and supplies were no longer sent to the California missions.

▲

A view of the inside of the mission.

Fray Ibáñez was laid to rest at the mission.

The Decline of Mission Nuestra Señora de la Soledad

Fray Sarría

A friar named Vincente Francisco de Sarría came to live at the mission after Fray Ibáñez died. Fray Sarría was a hardworking and caring friar. He had served for six years as the prefect of all the California missions. This meant that he worked with the mission president to make sure that all the friars were performing all their religious duties and living in the way that friars should. He worked to make sure that the friars followed the oath of poverty that they had all taken when they became Franciscans. He wanted them to remember that even if their missions were successful, the wealth that they produced belonged to the neophytes, not to the friars. He made sure that the friars' rooms were not too large and that their furniture was not too nice. He had all the friars wear habits as a sign of poverty. He also reminded the friars that they were responsible for learning the language of the California Indians at their mission, and that religious instruction should be given in those languages, not in Spanish.

Fray Sarría had become the mission prefect in 1812, and in 1818 he voluntarily quit his powerful position just so he could work at Mission Soledad.

Floods

In 1824, severe flooding damaged the church and the sacristy. The neophytes repaired the church immediately. The sacristy was rebuilt the next year. In 1832, another flood destroyed the restored church. Fray Sarría wrote a letter to Mexican officials saying that a temporary church had been built because the other one had "tumbled down." The mission buildings were almost entirely ruined.

Today, Mission Soledad has been restored and serves as a reminder of California's rich and interesting past. ▶

The Neophytes Leave

With the mission in such terrible shape, many neophytes began to leave. In addition, the Mexican government decided they wanted to secularize the missions. This meant that the friars would no longer have control over the neophytes or over the mission lands. The mission lands would be under the control of the Mexican government, and the neophytes would live there as tax paying Mexican citizens. When the neophytes at Mission Nuestra Señora de la Soledad heard that they would soon be free, even more of them left the mission.

With so few neophytes at the mission, there were not enough people there to do all the work needed to grow crops. Food became scarce, and many of the people still left at the mission became weak and sick.

On May 24, 1835, Fray Sarría died on a Sunday morning while celebrating Mass in the church at Mission Soledad. Because the mission was so poor, many people believe that he died of starvation. The remaining neophytes carried his body to Mission San Antonio de Padua, where he was buried. After Fray Sarría's death, very few neophytes returned to the mission. No more friars were sent to Mission Nuestra Señora de la Soledad.

Secularization

It had been the original plan of the government in New Spain to turn the missions over to the American Indians after 10 years of mission life. This was never done, because the friars did not believe that the neophytes were ready to assume full responsibility for the missions. When

After the floods, the mission was severely damaged. This site was once the workshop.

the missions were finally secularized in the 1830s, corrupt officials in the Mexican government sold or took mission lands for their own profit. In 1836, Mexican officials came to Mission Nuestra Señora de la Soledad to see how much valuable property was left. They found a vineyard, three *ranchos* (big farms) at San Lorenzo, San Vicente, and San Fernando, and livestock that included 3,246 cattle, 2,400 sheep, and 32 horses. There were only 172 Ohlone Indians still living at the mission. By 1841, there were only 70 Ohlone Indians at the mission, with 45 cattle, 865 sheep, and 25 horses.

In 1846, the Mexican governor Pio Pico sold Mission Nuestra Señora de la Soledad to a man named Feliciano Soberanes for $800.00. The

Gold Rush miners looking for gold in California.

land that rightfully belonged to the Ohlone Indians had been sold out from under them.

California Becomes a State

Mexico did not have a strong hold on Alta California for very long. In 1848, gold was discovered in Alta California, and men hoping to get rich flooded in from the United States. Alta California was quickly filling up with American settlers. The United States and Mexico fought a war over the territory called the Mexican War. The Americans won the war, and in 1850, California became the 31st state.

The Mission Is Returned to the Church

In 1865, President Abraham Lincoln signed a decree that returned all 21 missions to the Catholic church. There was nothing for the church to reclaim at Mission Nuestra Señora de la Soledad. The mission buildings and land were in ruins. The mission remained no more than a heap of rubble for almost 100 years.

▲
Artwork showing struggles during the Mexican War.

Mission Nuestra Señora de la Soledad Today

An Interest in History

As more and more Americans settled in California, they became very interested in the history of the land. They copied the architecture of the missions, building their homes with archways and tile roofs. This interest in California's history renewed people's interest in the missions. Groups along the west coast banded together and began restoring the mission chain.

Part of the mission ruins.

In 1952, a group of women known as the Native Daughters of the Golden West decided to restore the tiny Mission Soledad. When the restoration began, all that remained were piles of adobe dirt along with the front portion of the church. Everything else had been destroyed by weather and neglect.

The group built a chapel to look like the original, but they left the crumbling walls that surrounded the church. When the restoration was finished, the mission was handed over to volunteers who had agreed to

An inside view of the mission.

◀ *Much of Mission Soledad lay in ruins for many years.*

49

maintain the restored mission. The ruins of the quadrangle, some of the rooms, and the cemetery were left as a monument to the original mission. What is left of the original Mission Soledad can be seen, by itself among the fields and trees, standing quietly as it did so many years ago.

The mission altar after it was restored.

These windows at the mission were also restored. ▶

A cross stands tall at Mission Soledad.

A photo of the mission gardens.

51

Make Your Own Mission Nuestra Señora de la Soledad

To make your own model Mission Nuestra Señora de la Soledad, you will need:

supplies

styrofoam

corrugated cardboard

glue

dry lasagna noodles

reddish-brown paint

white paper

scissors

miniature flowers and trees

Directions

Step 1: Cut out an 18″ by 16″ cardboard base.

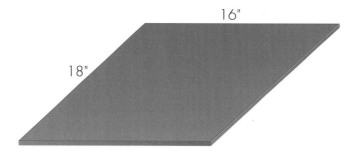

52

Adult supervision is suggested.

Step 2: Cut and glue together pieces of styrofoam to build the church walls. The front of the church should be 8″ by 6″.

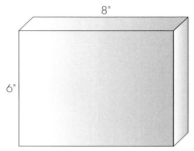

Step 3: Attach the front wall of the church to the base.

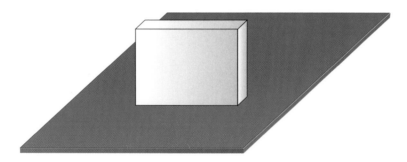

Step 4: Build each of the two side walls of the church so that they are 10.5″ by 6″. Glue to the base.

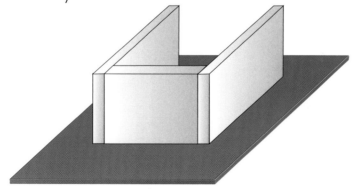

Step 5: Build the back wall of the church so that it is 8″ by 6″. Glue to the base.

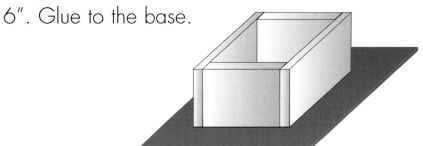

Step 6: Glue strips of white paper over the church walls to make them look as if they are covered with plaster.

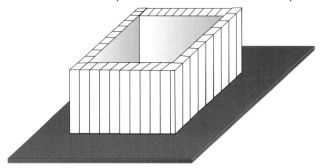

Step 7: To make the front door, cut out a 3″ by 5″ piece of cardboard.

Step 8: Glue the door onto the front of the church.

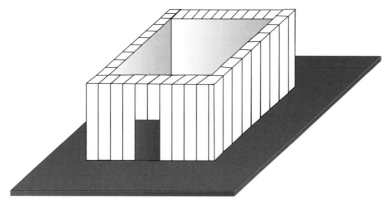

Step 9: To make a roof, cut a 13" by 11" piece of cardboard.

13"

11"   11"

13"

Step 10: Fold the cardboard in half, lengthwise, so that the roof will be pointed.

Step 11: To make roof tiles, paint dry lasagna noodles reddish-brown and let dry.

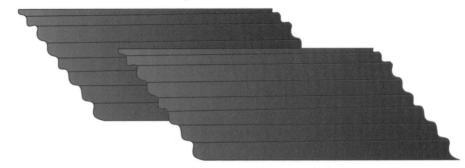

Step 12: Glue the painted lasagna noodles to the folded cardboard, and let the glue dry.

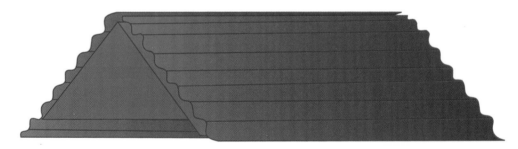

Step 13: Glue the roof to the top of the church.

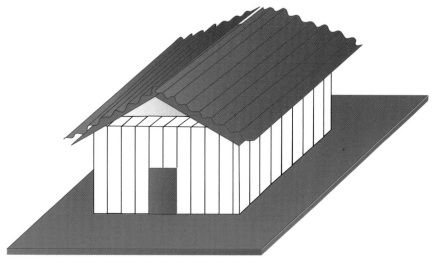

Step 14: Decorate the mission grounds with miniature flowers and trees.

*Use the above mission as a reference for building your mission.

Important Dates in Mission History

1492	Christopher Columbus reaches the West Indies
1542	Cabrillo's expedition to California
1602	Sebastian Vizcaíno sails to California
1713	Fray Junípero Serra is born
1769	Founding of San Diego de Alcalá
1770	Founding of San Carlos Borromeo del Río Carmelo
1771	Founding of San Antonio de Padua and San Gabriel Arcángel
1772	Founding of San Luis Obispo de Tolosa
1775–76	Founding of San Juan Capistrano
1776	Founding of San Francisco de Asís
1776	Declaration of Independence is signed
1777	Founding of Santa Clara de Asís
1782	Founding of San Buenaventura
1784	Fray Serra dies
1786	Founding of Santa Bárbara Virgen y Mártir
1787	Founding of La Purísima Concepción de Maria Santísima
1791	Founding of Santa Cruz and **Nuestra Señora de la Soledad**
1797	Founding of San José de Guadalupe, San Juan Bautista, San Miguel Arcángel, and San Fernando Rey de España
1798	Founding of San Luis Rey de Francia
1804	Founding of Santa Inés Virgen y Mártir
1817	Founding of San Rafael Arcángel
1823	Founding of San Francisco de Solano
1849	Gold found in northern California
1850	California becomes the 31st state

Glossary

adobe (uh-DOH-bee) Sun-dried bricks made of straw, mud, and sometimes manure.

aqueduct (AH-kwuh-dukt) A system of channels that carry water.

architecture (AR-kih-tek-chur) The art of designing buildings.

baptism (BAP-tih-zum) A ceremony performed when someone is accepted into, or accepts, the Christian faith.

Catholicism (kuh-THAH-lih-sih-zum) The faith or practice of Catholic Christianity, which includes following the spiritual leadership of priests headed by the Pope.

Christianity (kris-chee-AN-ih-tee) A religion based on the teachings of Jesus Christ and the Bible, practiced by Orthodox, Roman Catholic, and Protestant groups.

colonize (KAHL-uh-nyz) To settle in a new land and claim it for the government of another country.

convert (kun-VIRT) To change from belief in one religion to belief in another religion.

decree (dih-KREE) An official law or order.

Franciscan (fran-SIS-kin) A communal Roman Catholic order of friars, or "brothers," who follow the teachings and example of Saint Francis of Assisi, who did much work as a missionary.

friar (FRY-ur) A brother in a communal religious order. Friars can also be priests.

livestock (LYV-stahk) Farm animals kept for use or profit.

Mass (MAS) A Christian religious ceremony.

neophyte (NEE-oh-fyt) The name for American Indians once they have been baptized into the Christian faith.

prefect (PREE-fekt) An administrative official who worked with the mission president to make sure that friars were living and working properly at the missions.

quarters (KWOR-turz) Rooms where someone lives.

restoration (reh-stuh-RAY-shun) Working to return something, such as a building, to its original state.

sacristy (SA-kruh-stee) A room in a church where sacred objects and garments are kept.

secularization (sehk-yoo-luh-rih-ZAY-shun) When the operation of the mission lands was turned over to the Christian Indians.

shaman (SHAH-min) Medicine men who use magic to heal the sick and to control other events in people's lives.

thatch (THACH) A covering for a house made up of reeds and grass bundled together.

tule (TOO-lee) Reeds used by the Indians to make houses and boats.

vestments (VEST-mints) Robes that are worn for special ceremonies.

viceroy (VYS-roy) A governor who rules and acts as the representative of the king.

villages (VIH-lih-jiz) Original communities where American Indians lived before the arrival of the Spanish. Non-Christian, or non-mission, Indians continued to live in these villages.

Pronunciation Guide

atole (ah-TOH-lay)

camposanto (kahm-poh-SAHN-toh)

convento (kahn-VEN-toh)

El Camino Real (EL kah-MEE-noh ray-al)

fiestas (fee-EHS-tahs)

monjerío (mohn-hay-REE-oh)

Ohlone (oh-LOH-nee)

pozole (poh-ZOHL-ay)

ranchería (rahn-cher-EE-a)

ranchos (RAHN-chohs)

siesta (see-EHS-tah)

soledad (so-luh-DAD)

Resources

To learn more about the California missions, check out these books and Web sites:

Books

Genet, Donna. *Father Junípero Serra: Founder of the California Missions*. Springfield, NJ: Enslow Publishers, 1996.

Hogan, Elizabeth, ed. *The California Missions*. Menlo Park, CA: Sunset Publishing, 1991.

Keyworth, C. L. *The First Americans: California Indians*. New York, New York: Facts on File, 1991.

Young, Stanley. *The Missions of California*. San Francisco, CA: Chronicle Books, 1998.

Van Steenwyk, Elizabeth. *The California Missions*. New York, NY, Franklin Watts, 1995.

Rickman, David. *California Missions*. New York, NY, Dover, 1992.

California Missions. Santa Barbara, CA, Bellerophon Books, 1997.

Web Sites

http://www.escusd.k12.ca.us/MissionTrail.html
http://www.ca-missions.org/links.html

Index